1978

To Mike, Ron, and El[...]
With my best wishes for
Happy FUN reading!
    Pegge Dillingham

SOUND COMICS
SOUND COMICS
SOUND COMICS
SOUND COMICS

by
Pegge Dillingham

illustrated by
Claudia Fregosi

Prentice-Hall, Inc., Englewood Cliffs, New Jersey

Copyright © 1978 by Margaret Dillingham
Illustrations copyright © 1978 by Claudia Fregosi

All rights reserved. No part of this book may be
reproduced in any form or by any means, except for
the inclusion of brief quotations in a review,
without permission in writing from the publisher.

Printed in the United States of America.

Prentice-Hall International, Inc., London
Prentice-Hall of Australia, Pty. Ltd., North Sydney
Prentice-Hall of Canada, Ltd., Toronto
Prentice-Hall of India Private Ltd., New Delhi
Prentice-Hall of Japan, Inc., Tokyo
Prentice-Hall of Southeast Asia Pte. Ltd., Singapore

10 9 8 7 6 5 4 3 2 1

Library of Congress Cataloging in Publication Data

Dillingham, Pegge.
  Sound comics.

  SUMMARY: Sixteen short stories told as tongue
twisters including "Benje's Bakery" and "The Zany Zoo."
  1. Short stories. 2. Tongue twisters
I. Fregosi, Claudia. II. Title.
PZ7.D57913SO   E   77-28544
ISBN 0-13-823013-7

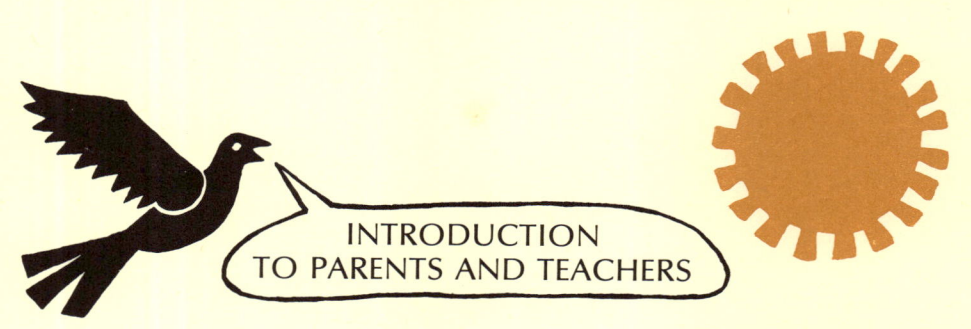

INTRODUCTION TO PARENTS AND TEACHERS

Transfer of corrected sounds into automatic speech through stabilization is an important step in the final stages of Speech Therapy. By this time the student has achieved a correct sound production in isolation, syllables, and words. He is now ready for methods that incorporate this correction in conversational speech. He will also have attained some reading proficiency to utilize exciting, humorous, fun-type practice material. These Sound Stories originated for that purpose.

The stories also provide entertainment, vocabulary enrichment, and opportunities for role play. All children (even those *not* enrolled in Speech Therapy) enjoy the stories as supplementary reading and the contextual cues facilitate word recognition and comprehension. The delight of the phonemic concept (the "sound of the sounds") provides pleasant auditory and kinesthetic experiences and facilitates the discrimination and production of certain phonemes and graphemes. The pure fun of these stories makes them a popular segment of any Speech Correction and/or Reading Program.

The illustrations were designed in comic-frame format to reinforce left to right eye movement and provide motivation for young readers.

The stories appear in the order of normal emergence of sounds according to "A Comparative Study of Articulation Acquisition," by Phyllis B. Arlt and Marjorie Tylke Goodban. *Language Speech and Hearing Services in Schools,* Vol. VII, No. 3, July 1976.

NATHAN NOBODY

Nathan knocked his knee on a nasty nail while trying to knot his necktie for the ninth time.

"Nuts, I'm just a knock-kneed nobody."

"Nonsense! You are nice: not too noisy and never naggy and nobody knows numbers like you do!"

Nathan felt neat as Nancy nattily knotted his necktie!

HENRY HUBERT

Henry Hubert hated to leave his hideout to hurry home.
He heard a horrible noise as a helicopter hovered overhead.

It landed nearby and out hopped Aunt Harriet who hugged Henry hard.

"Whooppee!
Now the wind will work my *windmill* to bring *water* from the well,

for my *sheep* who will grow wool,

that is wound through a *carder*,

and wheeled in a *spinner*,

and *woven* by weavers into worsted for workers to sell for our wealth!"

Benjamin Brown's Boston Bakery was between the bank and the bootery. Each morning bankers and businessmen bought butterbuns, brownies and bismarks for coffee breaks.

BENJE'S BAKERY

Very early one morning a bus load of hungry bandboys bought all the butterbuns, brownies, bismarks, banana bread, buttermilk biscuits, berry pies, and butterscotch bars.

Oh bother!

Have a free bite of my Boston Brown Bread.

This bread is a bargain. We'll buy it all!

Benje's Bakery was soon bare so Benje bolted the door and went bowling.

GHOST GRETA AND GILBERT GOBLIN

Ghost Greta crept away from ghosting practice to meet her friend Gilbert Goblin by the green gate.
Great Ghost glided after her and growled angrily.

Get back to your scaring lessons.

I want to learn goblin spooking.

Great Ghost grabbed for Greta grunting.

Greta dodged and grinned as Great Ghost fell into the gutter.

Don't be ghoulish.

Then she gaily galloped off with Gilbert to Goblinville.

THE YOKEL'S YAK

In yonder Yukon canyon lived a yellow yak who could do yoga while yodeling. A Yankee yeoman yearned to own the yak. The yak's owner, a yokel from Yorktown, said,

"My yak consumes a million *yams*, a billion *yogurts*, and a trillion *yucca plants* yearly."

Hearing that, the yeoman's yen for the yak was gone.
He sailed away in his yacht leaving the yak yodeling and yowling.

FRENCH FRIES

Floyd and his Father went fishing on Friday.
They fixed their favorite food, french fries and fruit, for snacking.
First Floyd caught three fish and Father caught two.
Then the fish stopped biting.

Floyd felt hungry and fiddled with the food hamper.
He fumbled around, spilling the french fries!
They fell into the water and floated down, looking like funny fidgety worms.

Suddenly the fish jumped!
Father caught five and Floyd caught four.
There were fourteen fish flip-flopping on the boat floor.
At five o'clock the fishermen went home to have a family fish-fry.

"However did you catch so many fish?" asked mother, when she brought in a platter heaped with french fries.
Floyd and his father nearly fainted from laughing!

VERONICA'S VALENTINE PARTY

Veronica, the lovely movie star, gave a Valentine party on her villa veranda overlooking the river valley.
Grapevine punch and vanilla cookies were served to a variety of guests.

Victor, the violinist, played waltzes.

Vincent, the voluble poet, recited verses.

But Van, the ventriloquist, was a villain!

He made vexing sounds with his voice while Vic and Vin entertained the guests.

Veronica told Van to vamoose—and Van vanished!

SANDY'S SPECIAL

Sandy works at the South Street Soda Shop.
Her strawberry and sasparilla sodas are scrumptious.

One day the supply truck got stuck and couldn't deliver the flavorings or fizzy water.
Sandy had only vanilla sodas to sell.
Disappointed faces, sad words, and sobs made Sandy sorry.

So she experimented, and mixed up a super new taste!
She stirred cider into the vanilla soda and added cinnamon stick candy straws.
Sandy sold her "special" for seven cents less than other sodas.

It was an instant success! Soon everyone was sipping Sandy's cinnamon-cider sodas through stick-candy straws!

LANCE THE DANCER

Prince Lance lived in a nice palace. He liked to dance and was known as Lancer the Dancer.
Whenever his friend, pretty-face Grace, came to visit he said,

"Let's dance!"

They were dancing in the fencing room when suddenly, Alice, the mouse of the house, appeared. Grace chased Alice throughout the palace, from attic to cellar.

But Alice escaped into the ceiling.

Lance sent for a special cat from France.
That made Alice prance!

Thereafter Grace and Lance practiced their dancing in peace.

Seizing their chance while Charlena chased around on her broom, the witches pitched her food into a ditch.

They chuckled when Charlena chugged off in search of food. Inch by inch she grew thinner. Her pouch disappeared. Her triple chin vanished.

Her double chin became one and Charlena was a charmingly changed witch!

GENTLE GIANT GEORGE JUNIOR

"I jog as I joke."

"The gymnasium will be your office."

Gentle giant George Junior lived in a gigantic castle. He joked and jogged and this jarred the giant king who sent George out to find a job.

George jogged around for a job. In one village his jokes made mad, bad and sad people, glad, gay and good! Jolly Mayor Joy offered George the job of Village Joker.

Each day people journeyed to the gym for joking and jogging with the gentle giant. Mayor Joy was just delighted with her jumping, jivey village!

LILLIAN'S LAMB

Lillian took her leaping lamb to the library.
People looked alarmed as the lamb *baaed* and leaped around the book stacks.
The librarian laughed and said,

Your lamb is likeable but lambs are not allowed in the library.

Lillian led her lamb to the lawn for lunch.
The lamb gobbled Lillian's *lettuce sandwich*, licked her *licorice lollipop* and flipped over her *lemon pie*.
Finally Lillian said,

Get lost, Lamb!

Lillian learned a lesson that lambs are not welcome at either libraries or lunches.